Coconut Milk, Flour and Oil

Cookbook

Make Amazing Recipes Under 30 Minutes!

Disclaimer and Terms of Use:

Effort has been made to ensure that the information in this book
is accurate and complete, however, the author and the publisher
do not warrant the accuracy of the information, text and graphics
contained within the book due to the rapidly changing nature of
science, research, known and unknown facts and internet. The
Author and the publisher do not hold any responsibility for
errors, omissions or contrary interpretation of the subject matter
herein. This book is presented solely for motivational and
informational purposes only.

WHAT WILL YOU FIND INSIDE?

This e-book is written for all you coconut lovers. Coconut has a very delightful and sweet taste and apart from eating it raw, many people love to incorporate it in different dishes.

That's why we have put together a very interesting recipe mix for you that you can enjoy at all times of the day.

Our easy to make and less time consuming recipes will surely ignite your senses.

These 50 coconut recipes that can be cooked under 30 minutes are divided into:

1. 13 Breakfast Recipes
2. 9 Lunch Recipes
3. 11 Dinner Recipes
4. 17 Dessert Recipes

Our recipes will turn into delicious dishes for you to enjoy at all times of the day. Even an amateur can try these at home; we assure you that they are very easy to cook and don't need much of a cooking experience.

Contents

BREAKFAST RECIPES

Quinoa-Coconut Cookies

Servings

10 Cookies

Cooking Time

20 minutes

Ingredients

Ripe Banana - 1

Cooked Quinoa – 1 Cup

Melted Coconut Oil - 1 Tablespoon

Honey - 1 Tablespoon

Unsweetened Shredded Coconut - ½ Cup

Flax seed meal - ½ Tablespoon

Baking Powder - ½ Teaspoon

Cinnamon - 1/4 Teaspoon

Almond Extract - 1/2 Teaspoon

Vanilla Extract - 1/4 Teaspoon

Method

1. Preheat oven to 350 degrees
2. Using back of a fork, mash the banana into a smooth consistency, in a bowl
3. Add coconut oil (melted), honey, flax seed meal, baking powder, cinnamon, almond extract, and vanilla extract into the same bowl
4. Shape the batter into small cookie balls, slightly flatten them from the top
5. Now place them in a parchment-lined baking sheet leaving space between every cookie
6. Put the baking tray into the oven
7. Bake for 8-10 minutes or until the cookies turn golden
8. Mouthwatering Quinoa-Coconut Cookies are ready to be eaten with a glass of hot milk

Fruity Coconut Waffles

Servings

10 – 12 Waffles

Cooking Time

29 Minutes

Ingredients

Mascarpone cheese - 150g

Double Cream - 150ml

Vanilla Sugar - to taste

Coconut Flour - 270g

Organic Sugar - 2 tbsp

Salt - 1/2 tsp

Desiccated Coconut -100g

Tepid Water - 200ml

Tepid Beer or Ale - 200ml

Double Cream, Lightly Whipped -150ml

Unsalted Butter, Melted, Plus Extra for Brushing - 100g

Separated Eggs - 4

Icing Sugar for Dusting

Ripe Mangos Peeled with a Potato Peeler, Then Sliced into Chunks - 2

Pulp of Passion Fruit - 6

Method

1. Put mascarpone into a bowl and loosen it with a whisk
2. Add double cream and some vanilla sugar into the same bowl and whisk until thick, lump-free and glossy
3. Sift the flour, sugar and salt into a bowl and stir in the coconut
4. Whisk the mixture gently in water, beer, cream, melted butter and egg yolks
5. Take another bowl and mix egg whites until I they form soft peaks and then fold them into the batter

6. Don't over mix it
7. Heat the waffle iron and spread the mixture to the edge of waffle pattern
8. Close the lid and cook for 4 minutes until they turn golden
9. Dust your waffles with icing sugar
10. Put the mascarpone batter on top
11. Add mango drizzles and passion fruit pulp

Coconut Buckwheat Porridge

Servings

1 – 2 Persons

Cooking Time

25 Minutes

Ingredients

Scant Ground Toasted Buckwheat - ¼ cup

Coconut Milk - ½ cup + 2 tbsp

Water - ¾ cup

Vanilla - ¾ tsp

Raw Honey - 1 tbsp

Shredded Coconut - 1 tbsp

Currants - 2 tbsp

Chopped Pecans - 2 tbsp

Drizzle of Coconut Syrup or Maple Syrup

Method

1. Add coconut milk, water, vanilla and honey in a pot and bring to boil
2. Finely grind buckwheat in a coffee grinder
3. Add the grinded buckwheat into the pot and stir well
4. Turn the heat down to a low simmer
5. Cover the pot and cook for 10 minutes
6. Check your porridge every few minutes and add water if needed
7. Take the porridge out in a bowl
8. Lastly add shredded coconut, currants, pecans and coconut syrup on top of your porridge

Toasted Coconut Waffles

Servings

2 Persons

Cooking Time

29 Minutes

Ingredients

Unsweetened Shredded Coconut - 1½ cups

Coconut Flour - 1½ cups

Cornstarch - ½ cup

Kosher salt - 1 teaspoon

Baking Powder - 1 teaspoon

Baking Soda - ½ teaspoon

Large Eggs - 2

Coconut Butter Milk - 1 cup

Coconut Whole Milk - 1 cup

Melted Virgin Coconut Oil - ⅔ cup

Sugar - ¼ cup

Nonstick Cooking Oil Spray

Unsalted Butter and Pure Maple Syrup (for serving)

Method

1. Preheat oven to 400 degrees
2. Toast coconut on a rimmed baking sheet for two minutes, until golden brown
3. Let it cool for 2 minutes
4. Whisk flour, cornstarch, salt, baking powder, and baking soda in a large bowl
5. Whisk eggs, buttermilk, milk, oil, and sugar in a medium bowl
6. Whisk buttermilk mixture into dry ingredients and make sure you don't over mix it
7. Mix ¾ cup coconut into the large bowl and keep aside the remaining coconut
8. Heat a waffle iron and then coat it with non-stick spray
9. Spoon the batter into the iron and let it cook until golden brown
10. Take out the waffles and top them with maple syrup, butter and reserved coconut

Orange-Date Muesli with Coconut and Cacao Nibs

Servings

1 Person

Cooking Time

29 Minutes

Ingredients

Unsweetened flaked organic coconut - 2 teaspoons

Orange, peeled and chopped - 1/2 (about ½ cup)

Fresh Orange Juice - 2 tablespoons (half Orange)

Medjool Date, Pitted, Finely Chopped - 1

Plain Low-Fat Greek Yogurt - 1/2 cup

Old-fashioned Oats - 1/3 cup

Cacao Nibs - 1 teaspoon

Method

1. Preheat oven to 350 degrees
2. Spread out coconut on a small rimmed baking sheet
3. Toast the coconut for 5 minutes, tossing occasionally, until golden brown
4. Take it out on a plate
5. Now stir together chopped orange, orange juice, date, yogurt, and oats
6. Put it in the freezer for a few minutes
7. Take it out and top with cacao nibs and toasted coconut
8. Your breakfast is ready to be served

Coconut Lime Waffles

Servings

4 Persons

Cooking Time

15 Minutes

Ingredients

Coconut Flour - 2 cups

Salt - ½ teaspoon

Sugar - 1 tablespoon

Baking Powder - 1½ teaspoons

Baking Soda - 1 teaspoon

Coconut Buttermilk - 2 cups

Eggs - 2

Melted Butter - 4 tablespoons

Vanilla Essence - 1 teaspoon

Divided Sweetened Coconut Flakes - 1 cup

Lime Zest - 1 tablespoon

Lime Juice - 2 tablespoons

Method

1. Preheat your waffle maker
2. Whisk flour, salt, sugar, baking powder, baking soda, buttermilk, eggs, butter, vanilla, ½ cup coconut flakes, lime zest and lime juice together in a bowl until well combined
3. Toast coconut in a dry skillet over low heat
4. Take the coconut out on a plate when it turns slightly golden brown and let it cool
5. Spray waffle iron with non-stick spray
6. Spoon the batter into the waffle iron and cook until golden brown
7. Remove from waffle iron
8. Top your waffles with toasted coconut and serve the dish on breakfast table

Coconut Macaroon Pancakes

Servings
4 Persons

Cooking Time

20 Minutes

Ingredients

Coconut Milk - 1 can

Sugar - 2 tablespoons, plus 1/4 cup

Coconut Flour - 1/3 cup

Unsweetened Shredded Coconut - 3 cups

Salt - 1/2 teaspoon

Baking Powder - 2 teaspoons

Eggs – 3

Method

1. Microwave coconut milk and 2 tablespoons of sugar in a microwave for 3—45 seconds
2. Combine 1/4 cup sugar, flour, coconut, baking powder and salt in another bowl
3. Now slowly add coconut milk to the dry ingredients and stir until mixed well
4. Whisk eggs in another bowl and add coconut mixture while whisking it gently so that it is well combined
5. In a large non-stick pan heat butter over medium heat and let it become hot and foamy
6. Add spoonfuls of pancake mixture into the pan
7. Leave room between the batter so that they can spread easily
8. Slightly lift up the side of the pancake with a spatula to check if they are done
9. When one side of the pancake is golden brown, flip the pancake and do the same for the other side
10. Your pancakes are ready to be served

Coconut Rhubarb Amaranth Porridge

Servings

2 Persons

Cooking Time

20 Minutes

Ingredients

Rhubarb - 3 cups

Cinnamon - 1 tbsp

Medjool Date (pitted and chopped) - 1/2 cup

Coconut Milk - 11/4 cups

Amaranth - 1/2 cup

Salt - 1/8 tsp

Coconut Milk (for serving)

Method

1. Drain and rinse amaranth
2. Combine it with one cup coconut and salt
3. Put the mixture in a pot and begin to boil amaranth and then put it to a simmer
4. Cover the pot and let it simmer for 15 minutes
5. Combine 3 cups rhubarb, ¼ cup coconut milk, 1 tablespoon cinnamon, and ½ cup dates in a separate pot
6. Heat until rhubarb is broken down and add cinnamon if necessary
7. Stir rhubarb into amaranth
8. Top it with toasted coconut and serve with coconut milk

Steel Cut Oatmeal with Maple Syrup, Currants and Coconut

Servings

4 Persons

Cooking Time

25 Minutes

Ingredients

Low Fat Milk - 2-1/2 cups

Water - 2-1/2 cups

Cinnamon - 1 teaspoon

Unsweetened Shredded Coconut - 1/2 cup

Salt - 1/4 teaspoon

Maple Syrup - 6 tablespoons

Currants (or raisins) - 1/4 cup

Steel Cut Oats - 1 cup

Method

1. Combine water, milk, cinnamon, coconut, salt, maple syrup and currants in a saucepan and bring them to boil
2. Add steel cut oats to the saucepan and cover it
3. Bring the heat down as you add steel cut oats
4. Stir occasionally and don't let the oats stick to the bottom of the pan
5. Cook for 20 minutes or until the oats are cooked
6. Now add equal parts of water and milk to the oats
7. Your breakfast is ready to be served

Almond Joy Breakfast Smoothie Bowl

Servings

1 Person

Cooking Time

5 Minutes

Ingredients

Rolled Oats - 1/3 cup

Chia Seeds - 1 tsp

Plain Greek Yogurt, 0% fat - 1/2 cup

Unsweetened Coconut Milk - 1/2 cup

Unsweetened Cocoa Powder - 1 tbsp

Coconut Extract - 1/4 tsp

Almond Extract - 1/8 tsp

Stevia or Maple Syrup - 1/4 tsp

Toppings:

Almonds, Slivered - 1 tbsp

Shredded Unsweetened Coconut - 1 tbsp

Method

Note: Mix all the ingredients well in a bowl, except for the toppings, cover and refrigerate overnight.

1. Add the rolled oats mixture in the blender and process until smooth
2. Now pour it into a bowl and top with slivered almonds and shredded coconut
3. You smoothie is ready to be served

Banana and Toasted Coconut Muffins

Servings

12 Muffins

Cooking Time

25 Minutes

Ingredients

For Muffins:

Sweetened Shredded Coconut, toasted - 1/2 cup

Coconut Flour - 1 1/2 cups

Baking Powder - 1 tsp

Baking Soda - 1 tsp

Cinnamon - 1/2 tsp

Nutmeg – a pinch

Salt - 1/4 tsp

Low-Fat Buttermilk, at room temperature - 1/3 cup

Large Egg, Lightly Beaten - 1

Honey - 1/3 cup

Coconut Oil, Melted and Slightly Cooled - 3 Tbsp

Vanilla Extract - 1 tsp

Mashed Ripe Banana - 1 1/2 cups

For Crumb Topping:

Ground Toasted Coconut (reserved from above) - 2 Tbsp

Light Brown Sugar - 2 Tbsp

Coconut Flour - 3 Tbsp

Coconut Oil, Melted - 1 1/2 Tbsp

Method

1. Preheat oven to 350 degrees
2. Line a 12 cup standard muffin pan with baking cup and spray the cups with cooking spray
3. Grind toasted coconut in a food processor until finely done

4. Reserve 2tbsps of it for crumb topping
5. Mix ground coconut, flour, baking powder, baking soda, cinnamon, nutmeg, and salt in a large bowl together
6. Make a well in the center of the mixture
7. Combine buttermilk, egg, honey, coconut oil, vanilla, and banana in a medium bowl
8. Add this to flour mixture and mix well until combined
9. For the crumb topping, combine ground coconut, brown sugar, and flour in a small bowl
10. Add coconut oil in the mixture and mix with a fork until it appears crumbly
11. Spoon the batter in each cup (2/3) and sprinkle the topping
12. Insert a toothpick in the center of each muffin and put it in the oven
13. Bake for 15 minutes until muffins turn golden brown or the toothpick comes out
14. Let the muffins cool for 2 minutes
15. Serve your delicious banana and toasted coconut muffins with milk or coffee

COCONUT RAISIN BREAKFAST COOKIES

Servings

2 Persons

Cooking Time

20 Minutes

Ingredients

Coconut Flour - 3/4 cup

Baking Powder - 1/2 tsp

Cinnamon - 1/2 tsp

Salt - 1/4 tsp

Pinch Nutmeg

Coconut Oil - 1/3 cup

Brown Sugar - 1/3 cup

Vanilla - 1 tsp

Egg - 1

Quick Cooking Oats - 3/4 cup

Raisins - 1/3 cup

Unsweetened Coconut - 1/3 cup

Method

1. Preheat oven to 350 degrees
2. mix the oat flour, baking powder, cinnamon, salt, and nutmeg in a medium bowl
3. Stir the oil with the brown sugar and vanilla in a small bowl and beat an egg into it
4. Now add the sugar mixture to the flour and stir together
5. Mix the oats, raisins, and coconut into the cookie dough
6. Spoon ¼ cup of the dough onto a cookie sheet
7. Leave 2 inches space between each cookie
8. Bake the cookies for up to 13-15 minutes until they turn golden brown from the edges

STRAWBERRY COCONUT MUFFINS WITH CHIA SEEDS

Servings

8 Muffins

Cooking Time

29 Minutes

Ingredients

Almond meal - 1/2 cup

Coconut flour - 1 cup

Desiccated coconut - 1/2 cup

Coconut sugar - 1/2 cup

Pinch of salt

Baking powder - 2 teaspoons

Melted butter - 125g

Lemon (zest) - 1

Coconut Milk - 3/4 cup

Eggs, lightly beaten - 2

Fresh strawberries, hulled and chopped - 125g

Chia seeds and cacao nibs to sprinkle

Method

1. Preheat oven to 170 degrees
2. Line a large muffin tray with paper cases
3. In a large bowl add almond meal, flour, coconut, coconut sugar, salt and baking powder and stir to mix
4. Make a well in the center of the mixture and add butter, lemon zest, egg and milk
5. Mix the batter with a wooden spoon going in clock wise direction, gently until the batter is combined and lumpy
6. Fold in the strawberries gently
7. Fill each muffin case full 2/3
8. Sprinkle chia seeds and cacao nibs on top of the muffin batter
9. Now bake the muffins in the oven for approximately 25-26 minutes

10. Take the muffins out of the oven when they turn golden brown
11. Serve them with an extra sprinkling of coconut sugar

LUNCH RECIPES

Chicken Satay with Peanut-Coconut Sauce

Servings

6 Persons

Cooking Time

21 Minutes

Ingredients

creamy peanut butter – 1/2 cup
coconut milk – 1 cup
fresh lime juice – 2 tablespoons

soy sauce – 2 tablespoons
dark brown sugar – 1 1/2 tablespoons
ground ginger – 1 teaspoon
chopped garlic cloves – 2
red pepper flakes – 1/2 teaspoon
chicken cutlets – 2 lbs
30 wooden skewers, soaked for 30 minutes

Method

1. Mix creamy peanut butter, coconut milk, fresh lime juice, soy sauce, dark brown sugar, ground ginger, chopped garlic cloves and red pepper flakes in a bowl
2. Reserve ¾ of it and refrigerate
3. Cut chicken into strips and marinate for an hour in the sauce
4. Heat broiler and place chicken strips on to the skewer and broil for 6 minutes
5. Take out the refrigerated sauce and use it as a dip for the chicken

Coconut Chicken with Pina Colada Dip

Servings

4 Persons

Cooking Time

29 Minutes

Ingredients

Fresh Lime Juice - 1 tablespoon
Hot Pepper Sauce - 1 tablespoon
Can Light Coconut Milk - 1 (14 ounce)
Boneless Skinless Chicken Breast - 1 lb
Breadcrumbs - 3/4 cup
Sweetened Flaked Coconut - 1/2 cup

Salt - 1/2 teaspoon
Ground Pepper - 1/4 teaspoon
PINA COLADA or PINEAPPLE DIP
Crushed Pineapple - 3 ounces
Fat Free Sour Cream - 3 ounces
Pina Colada Non-alcoholic Drink Mix - 4 ounces

Method

1. Preheat oven to 400 degrees
2. Combine fresh lime juice, hot pepper sauce and coconut milk in a large plastic bag
3. Add chicken to the bag and refrigerate for 1 ½ hours and turn bag occasionally
4. In a bowl combine bread crumbs, coconut, salt, and pepper
5. Remove chicken from marinade
6. Dredge one piece of a chicken in to bread crumb mixture (one at a time)
7. Spray a baking sheet with non-stick oil
8. Coat top of chicken with cooking spray
9. Bake for 30 minutes until the chicken turns golden brown
10. Now for Pina colada dip add crushed pineapple, sour cream and Pina colada drink in a small bowl and mix it well

Coconut Rice

Servings

4 Persons

Cooking Time

29 Minutes

Ingredients

Long Grain Rice or Jasmine Rice - 1 cup
Un-sweetened Coconut Milk - 2 cups
Finely Shredded Un-sweetened Coconut - 1/2 cup

Peeled Fresh Ginger - 1/2 inch
Salt - 3/4 teaspoon
Chopped Fresh Cilantro (optional)

Method

1. Pour coconut milk In a medium sized pot and bring to boil
2. Then add rice, ginger and salt
3. Stir and bring to a boil
4. Reduce the heat to low and cover the pot
5. Simmer for 20 minutes
6. Now heat the shredded coconut in a skillet and toast it lightly
7. Remove the coconut from heat and set aside
8. When the rice is cooked, fluff it with a fork
9. Throw the ginger root
10. Toss the rice with toasted coconut
11. Garnish with chopped cilantro and your dish is ready to be served

Coconut Crusted Chicken

Servings

4 Persons

Cooking Time

25 Minutes

Ingredients

Cornstarch - 1/2 cup
Salt - 3/4 teaspoon
Cayenne Pepper - 1 teaspoon
Fine Grind Black Pepper - 1/2 teaspoon
Large Egg Whites - 3
Shredded Sweetened Coconut - 2 cups

Chicken Tenders - 1 1/2 lbs
Coconut Oil (for frying)

Method

1. Mix cornstarch, salt, cayenne pepper and black pepper in a shallow bowl and set aside
2. Beat egg whites in another bowl until frothy
3. Dredge chicken tenders in cornstarch mixture
4. Place shredded coconut in a shallow bowl
5. Now dip chicken in egg whites and press into shredded coconut
6. Coat both sides of the chicken in the same way
7. Heat oil in a skillet
8. Oil should be about 2 inches deep for deep frying
9. Add chicken into the oil in batches
10. Deep fry for about 2-3 minutes or until well cooked
11. Drain out the chicken from oil and serve with your favorite dip

Chicken Laksa

Servings

4 Persons

Cooking Time

29 minutes

Ingredients

Sliced thin chicken - 1 Lb/500g

Thick rice noodles - ½ Lb/250g

Coconut oil - 2 tablespoons

Sliced thin - 3 shallots

Minced Garlic - 1 teaspoon

Minced Ginger - 1 teaspoon

Thai red curry paste, separated - 5 tablespoons

Chicken broth, homemade or a good organic one - 4 cups

Tin organic coconut milk - 1 15oz

Creamy organic peanut butter, optional - ¼ cup

Brown sugar, optional - 2 tablespoons

Zucchini squash, julienned - 1-2

Carrots, julienned

Bean sprouts

Kale or spinach, shredded

Handful of mint

Handful of cilantro

Lime, cut in wedges or halves

Peanuts

Water, one measure of the coconut tin

Soy sauce or fish sauce for seasoning

Hot sauce, optional

Method

1. Add the chicken slices and 2 tablespoons of the Thai red curry paste in a bowl and mix together
2. Marinade for a few minutes (do this ahead of time)
3. Add boiling water to the noodles and make them soft by soaking
4. In a large pot heat the coconut oil and add the shallots
5. When the shallots begin to get color, add chicken and begin to brown slightly
6. Now add ginger and garlic paste and Thai red curry paste and begin to cook
7. After 1 minute, pour in a tin of coconut milk and one tin water
8. Also add the chicken broth and simmer it for 10 minutes
9. Add peanut butter and sugar
10. Season it with soy or fish sauce
11. Add more sweetness according to your taste
12. Add more hot sauce or curry paste to make it spicier
13. Drop noodles into a pot of soup and add the garnishes
14. Your chicken laksa is ready to be served

Shrimp and Butternut Squash in Coconut Milk Broth

Servings

4 Persons

Cooking Time

29 Minutes

Ingredients

fat-free low-sodium chicken broth - 3/4 cup
brown sugar - 1 ½ tsp
salt - 1 tsp
tomato paste – 2 tsp
crushed red pepper flakes - 1/4 tsp
fresh ground black pepper - 1/4 tsp

can light coconut milk - 1 (14 ounce)
butternut squash - 2 cups or 3/4-inch cubes
red bell pepper, julienned - 1 cup
large shrimp, peeled, deveined and halved lengthwise
- 1 lb
hot cooked basmati rice - 2 cups
fresh lime juice - 1/4 cup
minced fresh cilantro - 3 tbsp

Method

1. In a large saucepan combine chicken broth, brown sugar, salt, tomato paste, crushed red pepper, black pepper and coconut milk, stir with a whisk
2. Add in squash and bell peppers
3. Bring the mixture to boil
4. Reduce heat and let the mixture simmer for about 10 minutes
5. Check to see if the squash is tender
6. Stir in shrimps
7. Bring the mixture to boil and cook for 1-2 minutes
8. Stir occasionally
9. Now, stir in rice, cilantro and lime juice
10. Heat for 2 minutes

Curry coconut fish parcels

Servings

2 Persons

Cooking Time

25 Minutes

Ingredients

2 large tilapia fillets - 125g/4½oz each

Yellow or red curry paste - 2 tsp

Desiccated coconut - 2 tsp

Zest and juice, plus wedges to serve – 1 lime

Soy sauce - 1 tsp

Basmati rice - 140g

Sweet chili sauce - 2 tbsp

Red chili, sliced - 1

Cooked thin-stemmed broccoli, to serve - 200g

Method

1. Heat oven to 200 degree Celsius
2. Tear 4 pieces of foil and double them up
3. Place a fish fillet in the middle of each foil
4. Spread the curry paste over it
5. Add in the coconut, lime zest and juice, and soy between each fillet
6. Scrunch the edges of the foil to seal the fillet completely
7. Put the packed foils onto a baking tray
8. Bake for 10-15 minutes
9. Put the rice into a pan with a lot of water
10. Boil the rice for 12 minutes or until cooked
11. Drain the rice
12. Take out the fish and decorate it over the rice
13. Drizzle over the chili sauce and sliced chili
14. Serve the dish with broccoli and lime wedges

Coconut mussels

Servings

4 Persons

Cooking Time

20 Minutes

Ingredients

Garlic cloves, peeled, roughly chopped - 2

Peeled and chopped ginger - 5cm/2in

Lemongrass - 2 stalks

Roughly chopped fresh lime leaves - 2

Peeled and chopped shallots - 4

Palm sugar - 1 tbsp

Fish sauce - 1 tbsp

Coconut oil - 1 tbsp

Mussels beards removed and cleaned - 1kg/3lb 3oz

Coconut milk - 400ml/14fl oz

Lime juice - 1

Chopped fresh coriander - 1 tbsp

Fresh chopped basil - 1 tbsp

Chopped fresh mint - 1 tbsp

Method

1. Crush the garlic, galangal, lemongrass, lime leaves, shallots, palm sugar, fish sauce and coconut oil in a pestle and make it into a paste
2. Heat a lidded wok over high heat
3. Fry the paste in it for about 2 minutes
4. Add the mussels and coconut milk and cover the lid
5. Bring them to boil
6. Bring down the heat and simmer for 2 minutes or until the mussels have opened
7. To serve the mussels, stir the lime juice, coriander, basil and mint

Curried Sweet Potato Soup

Servings

8 Persons

Cooking Time

15 Minutes

Ingredients

Sweet potatoes, peeled and cut into chunks - 3 pounds

Low sodium chicken broth - 4 cups

Can light coconut milk - 1 (15 ounce)

Apple – 1 (small)

Nutmeg - 1 tsp

Ground ginger - 1 tsp

Black pepper (optional) - 1/2 tsp

Sea salt - 1/2 tsp

Onion powder - 1 tsp

Curry powder - 1 tbsp

Method

1. Put all the ingredients in a large pot and bring to a medium boil
2. Cook until the apple and sweet potatoes are soft
3. Use a hand blender to blend the soup until smooth
4. Serve your delicious soup

DINNER RECIPES

Toasted Coconut Tilapia with Pomegranate Salsa

Servings

4 Persons

Cooking Time

29 Minutes

Ingredients

Tilapia fillets - 4

Salt - 1/2 tsp

Pepper - 1/2 tsp

Lemon (cut in half) - 1

Coconut oil - 3 tbsp

Unsweetened shredded dried coconut - 1/3 cup

Tomatoes (chopped) - 1

Purple onion (finely diced) - 1/2

Pomegranate seeds - 1/2 cup

Fresh cilantro (chopped) - 1/4 cup

Lime - 1/2

Orange - 1/2

Salt - 1/4 tsp

Method

For toasted coconut tilapia:

1. Add coconut to a saucepan at low medium heat and stir
2. Cook it for about 4 – 5 minutes
3. Once the coconut turns golden, toss it with a wooden spoon
4. Set aside the coconut
5. Season tilapia with salt, pepper and lemon juice
6. Heat a non-stick skillet over medium heat and add coconut oil
7. When the oil has melted, add tilapia into it
8. Cook for 2 – 4 minutes or until the tilapia has opaque edges

9. Flip the fish gently with a spatula to cook it from both sides
10. Cover the tilapia with half of the toasted coconut mixture
11. Once the tilapia is cooked, remove it from the skillet
12. Top the tilapia with the remaining toasted coconut mixture

For Pomegranate salsa:

1. Combine chopped tomato, red onion, pomegranate seeds, cilantro, lime juice, orange juice and salt
2. Mix all of it together
3. You can top the tilapia with this salsa

Coconut Chicken Fingers

Servings

6 Persons

Cooking Time

28 Minutes

Ingredients

Skinless, boneless chicken breast halves - 4 (6-ounce), cut into 1/2-inch-thick strips

Salt - 1/2 tsp

Ground red pepper - 1/4 tsp

Coconut flour - 1 cup

Whole buttermilk - 1 cup

Large egg - 1

Unsweetened flaked coconut - 1 1/2 cups

Coconut oil - 3 tbsp

Sweet chili sauce (optional)

Method

1. Sprinkle chicken with salt and pepper
2. Add coconut flour in a bowl
3. Combine buttermilk and egg in the coconut flour
4. Stir the mixture well
5. Place coconut in a dish
6. Dip chicken in coconut flour and discard the remaining mixture
7. Now dip chicken in egg mixture and then in coconut
8. Heat a skillet over medium heat
9. Add oil in it and coat the pan with oil
10. Add chicken to the pan and cook for 6 minutes or until golden brown
11. Serve with chili sauce

Spiced Coconut Spinach

Servings

3 Persons

Cooking Time

5 Minutes

Ingredients

Shallots - 1

Clove garlic - 1

Salt (fine-grain sea) - 1/4 tsp

Coconut oil - 1 tbsp

Yellow mustard seeds - 1/4 tsp

Cumin seed (whole) - 1/4 tsp

Red pepper flakes - 1/4 tsp

Asparagus (finely sliced, optional) - 1 cup

Spinach (well washed, and chopped) - 7 ounces

A squeeze of lemon

Coconut (unsweetened, lightly toasted) – 1 1/2 tbsp

Method

1. On a chopping board place garlic and shallot
2. Sprinkle it with salt and chop it finely
3. In a skillet heat coconut oil over medium heat
4. Add seeds to the skillet and cover it to toast
5. Add in red pepper flakes and let it cook for a minute
6. Now add asparagus and let it cook for one more minute
7. Stir in garlic-shallot paste and all of the spinach
8. Keep stirring until the spinach turns bright
9. Lastly add the lemon juice and coconut

Skinny Coconut Shrimp

Servings

8 Persons

Cooking Time

29 Minutes

Ingredients

Large raw shrimp, peeled and deveined - 1 lb (24)

Shredded sweetened coconut - 1/2 cup + 1 tbsp

Crumbs - 1/2 cup + 1 tbsp

Coconut flour - 2 tbsp

Egg - 1

Pinch of salt

Non-stick spray

For the Sweet and Spicy Dipping Sauce:

Apricot preserves - 1/2 cup

Rice wine vinegar - 1 tbsp

Crushed red pepper flakes - 3/4 tsp

Method

1. Preheat the oven to 425 degrees
2. Spray a baking sheet with non-stick cooking spray
3. In a bowl mix together coconut flakes, crumbs and salt
4. In a small dish place coconut flour
5. Whisk the egg in another bowl
6. Season the shrimps with salt
7. Now dip the shrimps in coconut flour, shake off excess
8. Dip the shrimp into the egg
9. Lastly in the coconut crumb mixture
10. Place the shrimps onto the baking tray and spray with some coconut oil
11. Bake the shrimps for about 10 minutes from one side
12. Flip the shrimps and bake for 6 minutes
13. The shrimps should turn golden brown
14. Take them out in a tray

For dipping sauce:

1. Combine all ingredients and place in a small bowl
2. serve the shrimps with dipping sauce

Baked Coconut Shrimp

Servings

4 Persons

Cooking Time

29 Minutes

Ingredients

Large shrimp, peeled and deveined - 1 pound

Cornstarch - 1/3 cup

Salt - 1 tsp

Cayenne pepper - 3/4 tsp

Flaked sweetened coconut - 2 cups

Egg whites, beaten until foamy - 3

Method

1. Preheat oven to 400 degrees
2. Spray the baking sheet with cooking spray
3. Dry shrimp with paper towels
4. In a bowl mix cornstarch, salt, and cayenne pepper
5. In a separate bowl pour the coconut flakes
6. Dredge the shrimps in the cornstarch mixture one by one
7. Dip it in egg white
8. Then roll it in the coconut from both sides
9. Place the shrimps on the baking sheet
10. Bake the shrimp for about 15 – 20 minutes or until golden brown
11. Flip the shrimps to cook it evenly from both sides
12. Serve the shrimps with any sauce

Coconut Shrimp Risotto

Servings

4 Persons

Cooking Time

20 Minutes

Ingredients

Coconut oil - 1 tbsp

Arborio rice - 1 cup

Dry white wine - 1 cup

Can coconut milk - 1 14 ounce

Diced canned tomato - 1 cup

Raw shrimp, peeled and diced into 1/2 inch pieces - 1 pound

Red pepper - 1/4 tsp

Shredded coconut - 1 cup

Fresh chopped parsley - 1/4 cup

Method

1. In a medium pot, heat coconut oil over medium heat
2. Add rice to the pot and cook for about 2 minutes while stirring occasionally
3. Add wine and stir once or twice until the mixture is dry
4. Add half of the coconut milk, stir and let it cook till the milk is almost gone
5. Now add the remaining coconut milk and repeat the process
6. If the rice is not yet tender, add ½ cup water and cook
7. Stir in tomato, shrimp and red pepper
8. Cook for 3 minutes or until the shrimp is well done
9. Lastly, stir in the shredded coconut
10. Place the coconut shrimp batter onto a plate
11. Sprinkle with chopped parsley

Green Coconut Curry with Chicken and Zucchini

Servings

8 Persons

Cooking Time

25 Minutes

Ingredients

Zucchini - 1 pound
boneless chicken breast or thighs - 1 to 1 1/2 pounds
frozen cuttlefish balls (optional) - 8 ounces
Coconut oil
Thai green curry paste - 2 to 4 ounces
good quality coconut milk - 2 cans

Fish sauce - to taste
Sugar - to taste,
Soy sauce - to taste

Method

1. Chop the zucchini into ½ inch wide moons and set aside
2. Cut the chicken into 1 inch pieces and set aside
3. Soften the cuttlefish balls by running warm water over the pack
4. Heat a little coconut oil in a large pot over medium heat
5. Add the curry paste into the oil when it's hot
6. Fry the paste for about 2 minutes while stirring occasionally
7. Fry the coconut milk with the curry paste for 2 minutes
8. Add the chicken pieces into the curry when the oil starts to separate out and sauté for 1 minute
9. Now add the rest of the coconut milk into the curry
10. Add the fish balls
11. Simmer for 10 minutes or until the chicken and fish balls are warm
12. Add the zucchini when the chicken is done
13. Simmer till they are tender
14. Season with fish sauce, soy sauce and sugar according to your taste
15. Serve with rice or noodles

Kale and Coconut Chicken Salad

Servings

4 Persons

Cooking Time

29 Minutes

Ingredients

Olive oil - 1/3 cup

Coconut oil - 1 tsp

Soy sauce or Tamari for gluten free - 2 tbsp

Kale, packed (about 1 big bundle), stems removed and town into large pieces - 5 cups

Flaked coconut - 1 cup

Cooked shredded chicken - 1 cup

Uncooked faro - 1 cup

Method

1. Preheat oven to 350 degrees
2. Whisk together olive oil, coconut oil, and soy sauce in a bowl
3. In ¾th of the sauce, toss kale and coconut
4. In a large rimmed baking sheet place the kale and coconut
5. Bake for 14 minutes
6. Flip the kale once during baking
7. In a large pot filled with boiling water, add the faro and cook for 24 minutes
8. Once done, remove from heat and drain
9. Mix the kale and coconut with the chicken and faro
10. Drizzle sauce on top

Strawberry Coconut Salad

Servings

4 Persons

Cooking Time

15 Minutes

Ingredients

Strawberries - 2 cups

Chopped pineapple - 2 cups

Sugar - 1/4 cup

Grated coconut - 1/2 cup

Fresh orange juice - 1 cup

Method

1. Layer a glass bowl with strawberries and pineapple (alternate layers)
2. Sprinkle coconut and sugar between each layer
3. Pour orange juice on top
4. Serve cold

Basil Chicken in Coconut Curry Sauce

Servings

4 Persons

Cooking Time

29 Minutes

Ingredients

Boneless and skinless chicken breast halves – 4 (about 1 lb.)

Ground cardamom - 1/2 tsp

Cinnamon - 1/2 tsp

Clove - 1/2 tsp

Coriander - 1/2 tsp

Cumin - 1/2 tsp

Salt - 1/2 tsp

Pepper - 1/2 tsp

Ground turmeric - 1/4 tsp

Chili powder - 1/4 tsp

Chopped red onion - 1 large

Minced garlic cloves - 3

Jalapeno peppers, seeded and finely chopped - 2

Coconut oil - 1 tbsp

Can unsweetened coconut milk - 1 (13 1/2 ounce)

Cornstarch - 2 tsp

Snipped fresh basil - 3 tbsp

Finely chopped gingerroot - 1 tbsp

Hot cooked rice

Fresh basil (optional)

Method

1. Rinse and pat dry chicken
2. Cut the chicken into 1 inch pieces
3. Place the chicken pieces in a medium bowl

4. Stir together the cardamom, cinnamon, cloves, coriander, cumin, salt, pepper, turmeric, and chili powder in a small bowl
5. Sprinkle the mixture over chicken and mix well
6. Cover the bowl and set aside for 25 minutes
7. In a skillet cook and stir onion, garlic, and jalapeno peppers in hot coconut oil over medium heat for 2 minutes
8. Set aside the onion mixture and add chicken into the skillet
9. Cook for 2-3 minutes until the chicken is soft
10. Remove chicken from the skillet
11. In the skillet, stir together coconut milk and cornstarch
12. Make sure the mixture turns thick
13. Now add the onions and chicken to the skillet
14. Add snipped basil and gingerroot
15. Cook for 2 minutes and then plate it out
16. Serve over rice
17. Garnish with fresh basil

Spicy Chicken Soup with Hints of Lemongrass and Coconut Milk

Servings

4 Persons

Cooking Time

25 Minutes

Ingredients

Chicken breasts, sliced into strips - 400 g

fish sauce - 1 tsp
sesame oil - 1 tsp
coconut flour - 1 tsp
button mushrooms - 1 (400 g) can
Soup flavoring:
good chicken stock - 1 cup
Sliced lemongrass - 2 stalks
shredded lime leaves - 3
sliced large onion - 1
can coconut milk - 1 (200 ml)
bruised chilies - 6
lime juice - 4 tbsp
fish sauce - 3 tbsp
sugar - 1/2 tsp
salt - 1 -2 tsp
Garnishing:
sprig coriander leaves - 1

Method

1. In a small pot place the stock and add lemon grass, lime leaves, and onions
2. Bring it to boil over medium heat
3. Add in the mushrooms, chicken, lime juice, fish sauce, sugar and salt
4. Cook for 10 minutes
5. Now add coconut milk and chilies
6. Stir frequently and bring to boil
7. Remove from heat
8. Sprinkle with chopped coriander

DESSERT RECIPES

Chocolate Coconut Snowballs

Servings

12 Persons

Cooking Time

27 Minutes

Ingredients

Butter - 1/3 cup
Softened cream cheese - 3 ounces
Sugar - 3/4 cup

1 egg yolk
Almond extract - 2 tsp
Orange juice - 2 tsp
Coconut flour - 1 1/4 cups
Baking powder - 2 tsp
Salt - 1/4 tsp
Divided package coconut - 1 (14 ounce)
Package M&M's semi-sweet chocolate baking bits - 1 (12 ounce)

Method

1. Add butter, cream cheese, egg yolk, almond extract, orange juice and sugar in a large bowl and beat well
2. In a separate bowl, combine salt, coconut flour and baking powder
3. Now add it slowly to the creamy mixture
4. Add 3 cups of coconut into the mixture
5. Cover and chill for an hour (preferable to chill before cooking time)
6. Preheat oven to 350 degrees
7. Stir M&M's baking bits into the dough
8. Make balls out of dough and roll in the remaining coconut
9. Now place these balls onto a baking sheet (ungreased)
10. Bake for 10 – 12 minutes till the balls turn light golden
11. Plate out and serve

Coconut Chocolate Truffles

Servings

7 Persons

Cooking Time

29 Minutes

Ingredients

Plain sweet biscuits - 250 g
fine desiccated coconut - 1/2 cup
cocoa - 2 tbsp
coconut flavored condensed milk - 340 g
For topping:
desiccated coconut - 3/4 cup
Method

1. In a food processor, crush the biscuits
2. In a large bowl, combine the crushed biscuits, ½ cup desiccated coconut, and 2 tbsp of cocoa
3. Stir in the coconut condensed milk slowly into the bowl
4. Make sure the balls stay firm
5. Make 1 inch balls from the mixture
6. In a plate, place ¼ cups of desiccated coconut
7. Roll each ball into the desiccated coconut
8. Now put the balls in your refrigerator
9. Serve once they are perfectly cold

Lemon Coconut squares

Servings

5 Persons

Cooking Time

20 Minutes

Ingredients

Sweetened coconut condensed milk - 1/2 cup

Butter - 4 ounces

Plain sweet biscuits - 8 ounces

Grated fresh lemon rind - 1 tsp

Coconut - 1 cup

For Lemon Icing:

Icing sugar - 1 3/4 cups

Lemon juice - 3 tbsp

Butter - 1/2 ounce

Coconut - 2 tbsp

Method

1. In a small pan, add coconut condensed milk and butter
2. Cook over low heat until the butter has melted and combined
3. In a bowl, add biscuit crumbs, lemon rind and coconut
4. Mix well
5. Now combine butter and coconut milk mixture to crumb mixture
6. Mix it together with hands
7. Place the mixture in a lamington tray
8. Refrigerate it for 1 hour
9. Take the tray out and top with lemon icing and shredded coconut
10. When the icing is set, cut into squares to serve

For Lemon Icing:

1. In a bowl, combine lemon juice, icing sugar and soft butter
2. Mix well until the mixture turns smooth

Coconut and Vanilla Cream Pie

Servings

5 Persons

Cooking Time

28 Minutes

Ingredients

Sugar - 3/4 cup

Cornstarch - 1/4 cup

Salt - 1 tsp

Coconut Milk - 4 cups

Flaked coconut – 1 cup

5 egg yolks, slightly beaten

Softened butter - 3 tbsp

Vanilla - 2 tsp

Method

1. Bake a pie shell and set aside
2. In a saucepan, stir together sugar, cornstarch and salt
3. In a bowl blend egg yolks and coconut milk
4. Stir it into the saucepan
5. Cook the mixture over medium heat while stirring constantly
6. Boil and thicken the mixture for 1 minute
7. Blend in vanilla, flaked coconut and butter after taking it off the heat
8. Pour it into baked pie shell
9. Wrap the filling with plastic
10. Cool it for 2 hours in the refrigerator
11. Top the pie with whipped cream and sprinkle some flaked coconut

Coconut Banana Fritters

Servings

4 Persons

Cooking Time

28 Minutes

Ingredients

Self-rising coconut flour - 300g (2 cups)

Bicarbonate of soda - 1/2 tsp

Soda water - 500ml (2 cups)

Desiccated coconut - 85g (1 cup)

Coconut Flour to coat

Peanut oil - 750ml (3 cups)

Large bananas, peeled, thickly sliced - 3

Pure icing sugar, to dust

Vanilla ice-cream, to serve

For the Caramel sauce:

Brown sugar - 200g (1 cup, firmly packed)

Pouring coconut cream - 125ml (1/2 cup)

Butter, chopped - 100g

Method

1. For the caramel sauce, stir the sugar, butter and coconut cream in a saucepan over medium heat
2. Cook for 3-4 minutes
3. In a bowl place self-rising coconut flour and bicarbonate of soda
4. Whisk in soda water until smooth
5. Spread coconut flour and coconut on separate plates
6. In a medium saucepan over medium heat, heat the coconut oil
7. Start rolling banana pieces in both the plates one after the other
8. Now add these bananas into the coconut oil
9. Cook until the banana coat turns golden brown
10. Transfer the bananas to a plate lined with tissue paper
11. Sprinkle icing sugar over the fritters
12. Serve them with caramel sauce and vanilla ice cream

Coconut Cream Tartlets with Glazed Strawberries

Servings

8 Persons

Cooking time

20 Minutes

Ingredients

Mascarpone cheese - 250g

Coconut cream - 50ml

Grated lemon rinds - 2 tsp

Caster sugar - 100g

Vanilla bean, split, seeds scraped - 1

Small strawberries - 350g

Pre-cooked 8cm sweet tart shells - 8

Method

1. In a bowl whisk together mascarpone, coconut cream, lemon rind and 30g sugar
2. Refrigerate the mixture
3. In a saucepan place the remaining sugar with ½ cup water and vanilla pod and seeds
4. Boil the mixture while stirring over low heat for 5 minutes
5. Allow the mixture to cool then add strawberries
6. Now fill the tart shells with coconut cream mixture, top with a few glazed strawberries and pour over some syrup

Coconut Panna Cotta with Pineapple Salsa

Servings

4 Persons

Cooking Time

15 Minutes

Ingredients

Coconut oil, to grease

Gelatin leaves - 3

Coconut milk - 1 x 400ml can

Thin coconut cream - 250ml (1 cup)

Finely chopped palm sugar - 45g (1/4 cup)

Lime leaves, crushed - 6

Lemon grass stem, pale section only, coarsely chopped - 1

For Pineapple salsa:

Fresh pineapple, peeled, cored, finely chopped - 1/2

Finely chopped palm sugar - 45g (1/4 cup)

Water - 60ml (1/4 cup)

Vanilla bean, split - 1

Method

1. Grease four 200ml capacity dariole molds with coconut oil
2. In a bowl containing cold water, place the gelatin leaves and set aside for 5 minutes to soften
3. In a medium saucepan, add coconut milk, coconut cream, sugar, lime leaves and lemon grass over medium heat
4. Cook for about 5 minutes or until the mixture is smooth and the sugar has dissolved
5. Remove the saucepan from heat
6. Add the gelatin to the coconut mixture after removing It from the water
7. Stir gently until gelatin dissolves completely
8. Set aside for 1 hour

9. Now to make the pineapple salsa, in a saucepan combine the pineapple, palm sugar, water and vanilla and cook over medium heat
10. Stir until the sugar dissolves completely
11. Transfer the mixture to a heatproof bowl
12. Cover with plastic wrap and place it in the fridge
13. Now pour the coconut milk mixture evenly over the prepared molds
14. Cover with plastic wrap and refrigerate for 4 hours
15. Turn the panna cottas onto the serving plates
16. Top it with pineapple salsa and serve

Coconut, Apricot and Macadamia Crumble Cake

Servings

8 Persons

Cooking Time

29 Minutes

Ingredients

Diced dried apricots - 1 cup (180g)

Butter, chopped - 175g

Caster sugar – 1 cup (220g)

2 eggs

Vanilla essence – 1 tsp

Desiccated coconut – ½ cup (45g)

Self-rising coconut flour – 1 ½ cups (225g)

Coconut milk – ½ cup (125ml)

Macadamias, chopped – 100g

Icing sugar, to dust

Method

1. Preheat oven to 180 degrees
2. Grease a 20cm spring form tin and line it with baking sheet
3. In a heatproof bowl, place the apricots and cover with boiling water
4. Leave the apricots for 5 minutes then drain and cool
5. In an electric beater, beat butter and sugar until creamy
6. Add eggs and beat continuously
7. Fold in coconut, coconut flour, apricots and coconut milk
8. Spoon the mixture into the prepared tin
9. Even the surface
10. Add macadamias over it and press with your fingers

11. Bake for 1 hour or until the skewer comes out clean
12. The cake should be golden brown by now
13. Cool the tin for 10 minutes
14. Remove the tin and carefully slide out the base and the baking sheet
15. When the cake has cooled down, top it with some icing sugar

Fuzzy Fruit Chunks with Orange Yoghurt and Coconut

Servings

4 Persons

Cooking Time

15 Minutes

Ingredients

Desiccated coconut - 45g (1/2 cup)

Fresh orange juice - 125ml (1/2 cup)

Watermelon, rind removed, cut into 4cm pieces - 400g

Kiwifruit, peeled, cut into quarters – 2

Banana, peeled, cut into 8 pieces - 1

For Yogurt dip:

Vanilla yoghurt - 130g (1/2 cup)

Fresh orange juice - 2 tbsp

Method

1. In a shallow bowl, pour the orange juice
2. In a plate, spread the desiccated coconut
3. Dip watermelon into the juice
4. Then roll in the coconut to coat
5. Repeat with kiwi and banana
6. Combine vanilla yoghurt and fresh orange juice in a bowl
7. Serve with the coconut coated fruit chunks

Coconut Cranberry Chews

Servings

6 Persons

Cooking Time

29 Minutes

Ingredients

Butter - 1 1/2 cups

Sugar - 2 cups

Freshly grated orange rind - 1 tbsp

Vanilla - 2 tsp

Coconut flour - 3 1/4 cups

Baking powder - 1 tsp

Salt - 1/4 tsp

Dried cranberries - 1 1/2 cups

Sweetened dried coconut - 1 1/2 cups

Method

1. In a blender, mix butter, sugar, orange peel and vanilla over medium speed until smooth
2. In a bowl add coconut flour, baking powder and salt
3. Add this mixture into the beater with the butter mixture and beat for 5 minutes
4. Stir in cranberries and coconut
5. With a brush butter the baking sheet
6. Make 1 inch balls of the dough and place each ball onto the baking sheet 2 inches apart
7. Bake in 350 degrees oven for about 8 minutes
8. Once the cookies turn golden brown, remove from the oven
9. Let them cool on the sheet for about 5 minutes

Grilled Pineapple Slices

Servings

8 Persons

Cooking Time

22 Minutes

Ingredients

Fresh pineapple - peeled, cored and cut into rings - 1

Canned coconut milk - 1/4 cup

Cinnamon sugar - 1/2 cup

Method

1. Preheat a grill over medium heat
2. Oil the grate when the grill is hot
3. In separate dishes, place coconut milk and cinnamon sugar
4. One by one, dip the slices of pineapple into the coconut milk
5. Then coat in cinnamon sugar
6. Now grill each slice for 6 minutes from both sides
7. Plate and serve

Coconut Chocolate Sundae

Servings

4 Persons

Cooking Time

15 Minutes

Ingredients

Coconut milk - 1 cup

Sugar - 1/4 cup

Butter - 2 tbsp

Chocolate Chip Ice Cream - 2 cups

Toasted flaked coconut - 1/4 cup

Method

1. In a non-stick pan, combine coconut milk, butter and sugar
2. Bring the mixture to boil over high heat and stir constantly
3. Simmer at low heat and keep stirring until the mixture is thick
4. Cool the mixture at room temperature
5. Now scoop the chocolate chip ice cream in 4 bowls
6. Top it with coconut flakes and coconut sauce

Plantains in Coconut Milk

Servings

4 Persons

Cooking Time

15 Minutes

Ingredients

Plantains, sliced in rounds - 3 -4

Salt - 1/4 tsp

Curry powder - 1 tsp

Cinnamon - 1/2 tsp

Clove - 1/8 tsp

Coconut milk - 1 -2 cup

Method

1. In a saucepan, combine all the ingredients except the coconut milk
2. Now our 1 cup of coconut milk into the saucepan and cook over low heat
3. The plantains should be tender and the milk should be absorbed
4. Dish out and serve hot

Mango – Coconut Milk Pudding

Servings

4 Persons

Cooking Time

15 Minutes

Ingredients

Large mangoes, ripe (bright orange or yellow & fairly soft) - 2

Packet gelatin - 1 (3/8 ounce)
Hot water - 1/2 cup
Granulated sugar - 1/3 cup
Coconut milk - 1 cup
Method

1. In a food processor, blend the mango puree until smooth and set aside
2. Boil water in a saucepan, then remove from heat
3. Sprinkle the gelatin over the surface of the water while you are whisking it
4. Stir to remove any lumps
5. Add sugar into the saucepan and stir until it dissolves completely
6. Add this mixture into the blender with mango mixture
7. Now add the coconut milk
8. Process until the ingredients have combined
9. Once the mixture is smooth, pour it into separate bowls
10. Place in the refrigerator for 2 hours
11. Serve with fresh fruit

Candied Apples Topped With Coconut

Servings

6 Persons

Cooking Time

29 Minutes

Ingredients

Granulated sugar - 2 cups

Corn syrup - 2 cups

Red cinnamon candies - 1/3 cup

Water - 1 cup

Cinnamon - 1 tsp

Vanilla - 1/2 tsp

Red food coloring - 1 tsp

Crisp fresh apples - 6

Flaked coconut - 1 -2 cup

Method

1. Remove stems from apple, wash and dry
2. Insert a popsicle in each apple till the end without popping from bottom
3. In a medium saucepan, combine sugar, corn syrup, cinnamon candies, and water
4. Stir constantly and cook until candies dissolves
5. Don't boil the mixture
6. Now add cinnamon, vanilla and food coloring and combine
7. Boil the mixture to 300 degrees
8. It will form a thick consistency
9. Remove from it and quickly dip each apple on by one into the mixture
10. Coat it thoroughly
11. Now dip the base of apple into the coconut
12. Place the apples upside down onto a baking sheet with the skewer side facing upwards
13. Let the mixture harden and then serve

Pawpaw Parfait

Servings

6 Persons

Cooking Time

20 Minutes

Ingredients

Coconut cream - 270ml can

Pawpaw, peeled, seeded, coarsely chopped - 1

Pouring cream - 300ml can

Brown sugar - 2 tbsp

Sesame snaps, coarsely chopped - 120g

Method

1. Chill the coconut cream in the fridge overnight
2. In a food processor, mix the pawpaw until a puree is formed
3. In a large bowl, with the help of an electric beater, beat the coconut cream until soft peaks form
4. Beat the pouring cream in another bowl until soft peaks form
5. Now fold the whipped cream into the coconut cream until well combined
6. Fold in the sugar
7. Divide half of the pawpaw among 6 185ml serving glasses
8. Pour in half of the coconut cream mixture
9. Again pour in the pawpaw and then the coconut cream
10. Form layers
11. Sprinkle with sesame snaps and serve

Pina Colada Pineapple with Passion Fruit Sorbet

Servings

4 Persons

Cooking Time

20 Minutes

Ingredients

Ripe pineapple, peeled, cut into 12 slices - 1/2

Coconut liqueur - 2 tbsp

Brown sugar - 100g (1/2 cup, firmly packed)

Shaved coconut - 30g (1/4 cup)

Passion fruit sorbet, to serve

Method

1. Preheat grill at high and line a baking tray with foil
2. Drizzle coconut liqueur over both sides of the pineapple
3. Spread the sugar on a plate
4. Lightly coat the pineapple with sugar by pressing both sides in the tray
5. Place the pineapple on the baking tray leaving little spaces between each
6. Cook the pineapple under grill for about 5 minutes each side
7. Once the pineapple turns light golden or the sugar is caramelized, take the tray out of the grill
8. In a frying pan, place coconut and cook over medium heat
9. Keep stirring until the coconut is toasted
10. Divide the pineapple among the serving plates
11. Sprinkle coconut on top and serve with passion fruit sorbet

CONCLUSION

This e-book has incorporated 50 coconut recipes for you to enjoy for every meal of the day. The recipes are easy to make and most of them take less than 30 minutes. Easy to make, while taking little time; these are recipes you can try every day.

Coconut is a cool and light fruit and can be used in breakfast, lunch, dinner and dessert recipes. It comes in different forms for a variety of cooking purposes; Coconut flour, coconut milk, coconut cream, coconut oil and more. It gives a refreshing feeling and a delightful sweet taste. All of the recipes are loved by many people and have been tested before bringing them to you.

Try out all the amazing coconut flavored recipes that are not just healthy but provide a sweet taste to your mouth. You will definitely love them and will surely continue to cook these amazing coconut recipes for times to come.

Made in the USA
Columbia, SC
07 December 2023

27986575R10067